THE CHINAMAN

THE CHINAMAN

DAVID MAMET

THE OVERLOOK PRESS
WOODSTOCK & NEW YORK

First published in the United States in 1999 by
The Overlook Press, Peter Mayer Publishers, Inc.
Lewis Hollow Road
Woodstock, New York 12498

The following items have appeared elsewhere in a different form:
"Brittany Spaniel"—*Gray's Sporting Journal*;
"Hotel Atlantic"—*Grand Street*; "A Charade,"
"The Waterworld"—*Ploughshares*; "Labor Day," "Olympia,"
"The Pond at Twilight," "Bad Penny"—*Bomb*; "Va-etze"—*The Forward*;
"Two Colors"—*The New Yorker*.

Library of Congress Cataloging-in-Publication Data

Mamet, David.
The Chinaman : poems / David Mamet.
p.   cm.
I. Title.
PS3563.A4345C56   1999   811'.544—dc21   98-31821

Manufactured in the United States of America
Book design and type formatting by Bernard Schleifer
FIRST EDITION
1 3 5 7 9 8 6 4 2
ISBN 0-87951-897-9

FOR REBECCA

CONTENTS

THE CHINAMAN

A Victorian Painter

It pissed cold rain the whole time.
Fumes stank up the town
A frog washed out of the street and down.
Too tired by half. And the thick slime
Looked dead on his back.

Rain in the puddles on the canvas
On the century-old street.
You say the street is gone.
The street is present, but the painter has decayed.
The rain is gone.

We went to the Chinese.
And art is long.
And the study of art is long.
When we came down the stair
I dreaded it was dead.
But the life was there.
My heaving belly, my sore legs
My tired hatred of
The men who could not paint.
And all the vermin
Feeding off the garbage in the town.

Although we made love in it.
Although we met there
What stakhanovite effort
Could style the city quaint?

It's not the picture which we see —
One hundred years have passed —
And not the showgirl's reverie
As she strolls home
And not the rain on her way
But the stink of petrol,
The excesses of a final day.
Murderers at the Tory escapade
In the Park Lane,
Rough virus weather in a flat below grade.
Weakness in the lungs,
A pissing vicious rain in Camden.

N

Chinee.
ong,
er tea;
nkey's song
pain
de hot
s brain.

See my retainers' lot,
Who expiate the sin
Of their vile birth
Serving the Mandarin.
But what is our pride worth
Who stand as commanded,
Where doth the logic fail?
Some are conceived to heat the monkey's head,
Some to drink tea and to display the fingernail.

BRITTANY SPANIEL

Seven oaks ring my estate.
It has no name.
The shooting and the hunting,
A beloved dog and two
Days of drunk grief
At his demise are
Not commemorated in the
Scar in the old marquetry
Upon that desk where
The cigar burnt down.
Nor is he on the hill he roamed.
And the calm of no horses,
Neither the shade of White Oaks
Informs my knowledge of the land.
There is no memory.
Only the momentary evanishment
Of that undescribed
Figure in the marquetry; Which
We may suppose
Was a country scene.

SEPTEMBER

The weather will come down.
The Fall come on.
If you ain't got it done now
You best get it done.
Five cords of wood.
Five markers of the way to keep you warm —
All part of the one song.
"If you ain't got it done,
Best get it done."

Watch the sun, then,
In the way he run.
The folly of completion,
For who did not know all states are one.
If you have not achieved it,
Go and get it done;
Because the weather will come down.

You do require five cords of wood.
The sight of it will keep you warm.
If you ain't got it done,
Go get it done.

With Willa in Mount Auburn Cemetery

Would you prefer
An Eagle or a Buffalo, she said.
I put the choice to her.
I think an Eagle, she said.
Graves of the Union Dead.
Soft acid-pitted stones.
The Yankee names she read
Who spanned
The Reaper to the Aerodrome
Sick mid-Victoriana,
Over-decorated vaults
On which she danced
Death will atone
For all our faults —
That is the peace we feel.
And this was my appeal:
"When I am dead, it's you must lay my stone."

THE PEACE OF THREE GIRLS SLEEPING

for Willa, Linda and Catherine

You being undissuaded
Remain driven to elaborate
Depraved confusion
Into universal law.

Three young girls sleeping
In a quiet house however
Redound to the gentle credit
Of these interactions
You in your lack of faith
Are given to decry

One may persist
In obstinate
Claims of betrayal and abandonment
But to what end?

Bagpipes, Harvard Square

Well lost.
There is the honor of the pipes.
Any may be the last.
In that sweet throb
At its conclusion
See the death you sought
Apportioning reward.
Rest or rejoice —
Any may be the last.

EPITAPH. *MARCHIONESS* VICTIMS. LONDON.

He will move
Heaven and Earth in his way.
He will move the water.
One on one side of the dispute,
One on the other.
One on each side of the river.
Dear friends —
Rest in peace forever.

THE BLACK RAVEN

My love is like a raven
Black against a sky of gray
With cold in your bones
And the winter coming on
And the smell of snow on the way
The sun's going down
But you're walking home
And the warmth going to ease your pain
Like a jet black raven in the sky
My love is a bird of change.

My love is like a raven
Above a field cut low
And what she sees as she flies to the trees
No man is going to know
My love is a secret never told
And an omen to swear by
Like a terrible raven overhead
In the rolling autumn sky.

When the black night falls The Raven Calls
And bathes me with her sweet breath.
And the rough gray blanket weighs us down
Into a sleep like death.

My love is an autumn Raven
Above a field cut low
With the order of heaven pressing down

And the frost on the stubble below
And the wisdom of the men and gods
And the folly of the day
Is in the Swift black raven
Flying in a sky of gray.

A CHARADE

A piece of paper
Which appeared to be blank
But on which we see
Writing had faded.
"My first is of the
Possessive of those
Given to possession.
And my last, the finality
Of proposition.
In entirety I give
That which in three worlds doth live.
Ungainly in the two;
In all, long-legged beauty,
Much as you."
Upon the paper which had come to fade
We strain to see
An ancient charade.
Can you decipher me?

THE PANEL HOUSE

A mass
Of brown hair on a pillow
A curled shaving on a knife —
In opposition, all the rest of life.

How gently odd
Our laudable Cabal — to see
This screaming anarchy,
And to exult to die
Praising the Name of God

NEW YEAR'S 1990

The influence of the Old Year,
Long on the wane, is most done.
Went out on a Hunter's Moon,
A Hoarfrost,
Ice in the pads of the dog.
Two people
In the high bed
Put paid to
That old moon, worn harness, and
Cloth gone rotten.
—All misapprehension of
The world turned vicious through
Anappositeness.
Things as they should be:
Fifty degrees of frost,
One dark, half-sleeping woman
Pulled her man to her.
The old year,
Gone in prayers by the bed,
Three magic shots of the pistol,
Woke the dog.
There is no lesson in it,
But sleep, but-love, in the Morning it was done.

Sociopathia

What vicious insult to the young,
What interminable wrong,
What affront, capable of sundering —
Where one would loose the bonds of personality
Rather than bear that injury —
Which self, being dismissed,
Could neither curse nor bless
This obscene line of reasoning.

Vermont, January

Lord of fire, God of the sword
Three hundred American dollars reward.
Dog ran off yesterday afternoon
And I got to head down country soon.

God sent a Savior to cleanse our sins
And Jesus died for you and me
Bread and butter, bitters and gin
That we might sin with impunity.

The track of the plough around the pole
Cold bear sleeping in a snowy hole
The depth of the woods, the lure of the fair —
Cassiopeia in her easy chair.

Epigram

Never a false step
Since human nature was perfected
By the birth of Christ

Down to the present day.
No action on the way
But betterment

Has brought us to this pass.

SONG OF THE JEW

I would die where my grandfathers died —
In that country we were banished from.
Even knowing it was not our home.
We came to the New World and we throve thereby,
In the equivalent of heresy,
Fleeing the only home we ever saw
In the two wandering millennia,
Which is to say, the study of the Law.

I would die where my ancestors died.
Happy to live caught in a Holy War,
If that were to live in a holy sphere,
In countenance of those who went before,
Rather to rise to wealth and power here,
And to endure the envy or the fear
Of that comfortable race I live beside.

I would die where my brothers died.
As they have died six thousand years
In the rocky places pushing the black sky.
But I write in complaisancy,
In the hypocrite love of life-as-it-appears.
With a mind no ancient law has filled with bliss,
With a face no desert wind sears,
An outcast, self banished from the tribe
I elect and administer by bribe
And join the decadent of my race in saying this:
Perhaps I am what has been said of me.

Hotel Atlantic

I

The lungs, being the seat of sadness,
Which Victorian memories spew forth,
Occasioned by a weakness taken in that seat.

A malformed woman in a pen and lighter shop,
Fat German waiters
In a railway hotel — when I had come to smoke Tobacco.

A deformed woman who never
Sold me a lighter or a pen

They were smoking in there,
Short of breath,

They had a sign, what would I not give
To remember that sign.
German waiters in the
Clipper Room of
The Hotel Atlantic.
A crisp dinner roll,
A woman
Who was not a hat-check girl.

One could
Leap down the stairs leap down the landings
One jump to a landing and
Two landings to a floor,
One's lungs,

Ruined by various years of smoking,
Various sadness,
And tobacco lit with no
Celebratory lighter from
The shop with the unquestionably lost sign,
With the kind,
Mismade, misfeatured woman,
With the man who died,
With the fat, German waiters, with the
Elevator man — one had elected
One could not recall his name
No matter how one tried.

II

Nothing away; no, nothing
One could take away,
No more
Than that which had transpired before,
No other than
That which went on before,
In that soft trial to summon up
Wisdom from memory,
Steam from a cold cup.

OLEANNA

For, you see,
If we call it Oleanna,
If we pray sufficiently,
Then we need entertain no fear
Whatever our state be,
If we are in a state of prayer,
The Lord will hear.
As it is written in the chronicles.
A City of the Fair,
A life of righteous ease,
Virtuous length of days.
No guilt to mar these.
Nights in the Pineapple Bed,
Love in all her Ways,
Converse with the Dead,
If only we will pray.
If only we will name it Oleanna.

For Rebecca

I thought I knew
What love was
Before I met you
But I did not know.

Many years have passed
In the pineapple bed.
Clothes mended and torn
Four times we saw them paint
The music room.
Children were born.
We moved toward
Converse with the noble dead.

Back in that time
I did not know
What love was,
I saw in the, as I thought, random
Progress of the world
Only obscenity,
And wished to die.
That time with you
Instructed me
To bless the vision
Into which you have consigned us—
That more-than-suspicion of eternity
In preparation for which
You instructed me.

"NEITHER THE SONG NOR WOMAN"

Neither the song nor woman
Would be understood
Except they were possessed.
The knitted rug, the turned wood,
Love wrought these artifacts.
Each loves as he can.
Some are blessed
In the performance,
Some in the reception of these acts.

The woman, too, was wrought
To love. As much respect
Must be brought to her
As was due
The care which had gone
Into the construction of a song.

THE OLIVER

The spirit of the boy,
Bruised on the boundaries,
Memorialized the dispute.
Differing tongues and tags,
Brief-rescued from the past
Constructed that new
Temporary freehold of the intellect,
Before it rested,
Resubsumed into the general.

Fugitive Green, and then
The bumping walk along the woods.
The secret languages I have
Aspired to learn, or mastered.
On the boundaries, a stone which said,
"it is restored." Another stone
Marking the confluence of
Two warring warrants on the land.

A Poem

Seven-and-so-many are twelve.
That number is five.
The Great, and those unfortunates,
Resist the convolution of the myth
To the one end —
Reduced to cozen knowledge from history,
Who will not profit to learn
From misfortune.

APRIL

No weak-natured girl;
No self-accomplished task,
But love. A contrarian sweetness
When we both went 'round —
Back to the house for a suede jacket on
The cold High Street,
And April would not be an apricot.

April 1990

Held at arm's length
The sun was a hand's width
Above the trees. And dinner was at dusk.
There was a false dusk in
The gray blue clouds
And black glass on the water.
There was a gun in the shed
And a man envied
Two ducks on the pond
Their innocent, abbreviated life.

The Triumph of Gravity

A Three Part Poem of the Hotel.

ONE

The Plague year.
The hotel.
The suicide.
Old Billy Barcus wristcuffed to the radiator.
Hookers and the old men hawk their guts up in the lobby.
Upstairs little girls and boys come in from the suburbs,
took their mother's car, to suck each other's genitalia.
Old grease and the piss smell of too-weak coffee sits in one
side of the lobby.
Cooks with scalded forearms take a cigarette from out the
greasy spoon. They all are filthy. They are fat.
Their bellies barely rest inside their stiffened aprons.
All of them are spitting in the soup. Their bloated fingers
scoop the salads from the bins.
The sickened residents in Winter. Taken with the flu. With
fears.
At four a.m.
They go down to the restaurant in sweaters and scarves.
House slippers and cigarette.
They smell like zoos.
They smell like elephants.
The little children call downstairs.
The horse degenerates lay in the lobby. Years ago. On
Collins Road.

In Saratoga. Then, iced coffee and a club, some steak sandwich.

Now.

"The niggers killing them."

In alleys, in the real estate. Out by the track.

The women in their shawls. Smell like the fish of hell. They do not urinate. Their body takes their life and sweats it in their clothes. They have not had their clothes off in a decade.

You see on the headboards. Grease. Vitalis. Brilliantine of ages. Shine, the walls, around the doorknobs, near the window, marks of jimmies. Mexican musicians. Down the hall. The wilted lettuce in the garbage on each floor. The remnants of the hamburgers, the condoms. Catsup-covered sporting pages, magazines, the semen-covered fold-outs. Tissues filled with sputum of tuberculars.

They had a boy was handcuffed to the toilet for a while they took him out. The gamblers in the lobby said they knew. He could have stayed in there and bitten through his wrist. Perhaps he liked it.

The little baby.

The hanging bar inside the closet we heard the cuffs were past over the bar, he stood he could stretch his arms. They saw the chafe mark where he rubbed it on the wood. The rummies coughing. All night long. At twenty second intervals. In fugue motif. They make a deep sound in the chest. Like women coming.

The cook goes in the elevator. His arm yellow to his shoulder from the nicotine.

Women with the walker. With the hairnets, with the housedress like dead cattle partly flayed, you wonder why

the flies don't cluster on her, never go outside. One person
puts the newspaper inside the trash. Another takes it out.
Inside the hotel was the boy they'd bought him in Atlanta,
someplace, down in Mexico, he could not speak, the only
thing he knew was food and water and his genitals and
men inside the closet, moanings in adjacent rooms.
The blood. The sputum in the sand ashtrays, the wrap-
pers of the candy bars, the mucus on the elevator walls.
The cheap scent of the drugstores, empty pizza boxes
littering the hallway, stuffed halfheartedly into the
garbage cans, the smell of marijuana, knife fights in the
corridors, at four a.m. shrill screaming in half
Spanish/English, death, a woman's death or play, or fore-
play. Jim the shoeshine looks out, <u>Yassuh</u>, step right <u>up</u>
there. Yes. It sho <u>is</u>...mmm mmm mmm, the heat, the
radiators knocking, all dried lungs down in the lobby, all
the shuffling of tabloids, crisp, all weakened voices, swear-
ing, the Vodka and the cigarettes, a change in weather,
swearing at the fucking niggers, the waitresses, though,
she's good, though, I think. I think she might be good.
What do you think?
I think she might be good.
Yeah. I think so.
(Fucking niggers)
Niggers and the Jews.
(The niggers)
When I came here rent was forty bucks a month, you
could stay in the park all night, you'd stay out, you could
watch the sun come up. You stay out now, you know
what? Yeah, they'll kill you. That they will.
How are you feeling?
No, I don't feel good.

TWO

In that moment everything turned bad.
It turned to chemicals.
My teddy my teddy we tilt toward the window.
My father said we're almost done.
(We were almost home)
Life is a dream and it is over.
Almost done.
Down on the floor the porcelain tiles are so cool,
So comforting.
Small dirty octagons.
The bed tilts.
We have gone.
The pull of the window, we see through, as we have not
seen.
We were almost there.
I said: are we there?
(We are almost there...)
But I'm so cold.
(We are almost there)
I was sick.
It poured through my mouth on to the pavement.
It came through the window.
The water was warm.
I put my cheek on to the spigot.
It wasn't cold.
Daddy, are we home, I said, No.
No, we aren't home.
Although the tiles were cold, I was afraid.
The sidewalk is covered in slime from the restaurant.
They kept the boy in there when the cops came he

was simpering, a fawn, he'd go to clutch them by their
genitals the little English he could speak "could I make
you feel good?"
All the grease floats up, the grease smells, floor by floor as
we go down.
We had all sinned, and we saw each other in the elevator.
But there was no magic there.
This must be immortality. How can we know if we do not
die?

THREE

A nose full of blood.
The coffee made his head fry.
"What do you think it means my nose won't stop
bleeding?"
It was orange.
Everything was slick.
Life is a dirty table.
Don't come near me with that thing.
Unless,
If you have <u>license</u> to be here. If not:
Some dribbling down, you can call it pain.
"What is done has <u>been</u> done." We can't speak to that.
It was the juice that made me ill. I felt what it could do.
But we are not here.
We are not meant to be here.
With boils.
With food.
With blood that flows.
With <u>steam</u>, which is a mere reflection of the thing it
signifies.

"Our home is in the sun." Those things we find here —
and we find them for a reason — are too slick or sharp.
It causes blood to flow.
It is not real.
Nor either is the fuse.
And nor the broken glass.
The light is out and we must go.
Our home is in the sun.
How can we violate that trust,
Whose home is in the sun?

BILLY THE WEAZEL

the and now said billy the weazel

If I had thee by my side

What would I not joy to brave?
Four Hundred Pieces of a Scary Ride.

ZADOK THE PRIEST

When he had gone to his fathers
Then the thing was cleared.
Knowledge of form and secret processes
Availing nothing in the light of
Him who was born blessed and sent for another thing;
But surely those without it slept in righteousness —
Who to deny them?
Send them down to Sheol, the blood of seven orifices running,
Pooled on the floor, a figure, arguably,
And that shape Zadok the priest.

The sightless eye indeed. Black winked at nothing
Down in Sheol.
Whoever had thought what, and how they took it,
Who proceeded whom — what did it warrant,
When the time above was slight, and when the other endless?
When to posit a progression, the jejune pretension of that
    cadet mind,
The very substance of the prose gainsaid;
And who was consecrated, a subject of no distraction
For who lived to call it drole?

And who lived to record that Adonijah ruled the land
With splendor theretofore unknown
And wisdom which denied the name to wisdom which had
    gone before?
None but the priest. None but the patched man,
And none but Solomon, when that the King had gone down
    to the earth.

TREMONT STREET

Who, when it had passed, would say
The black bag was not borrowed at the restaurant;
or that a labored pleasantry
reduced or added strain
to the already strained day
following the hurricane?

Or find the restaurateur
False in his demeanor
Mixed of overwrought concern
And an assumed superiority?
No one who had not been there.

When the wind
Dashed the globe down in the street
When the rain fell
So perpendicular
As rain in a sketch beyond talentless.

As rain in a drawing
By one obsessed
Past the point of care
Or hope of the same
On the part of One
Not similarly mad.

A Poem. October, 1991

But could I have willed
The man into the room
No. Yes, or at what point
Certainly not from birth.

Certainly not from birth.
But then a vast reorganizing
And a potential reprieve.

A potential reprieve and then
A loss completely equal to the gain.
So thrilled to have been shet of
Pain that did not strengthen.

I could not have willed
The man nor his contemporaries.
He was not born there.
And positive to the pit
Rejoiced that I am not God.

Ten Plagues

There is an observed tendency of things
At some but not all points
To improve markedly
Before complete disintegration.
Regression To The Norm,
The furtive, momentary stop
Of a violent state of flux
Goes by the name of intervention.

While we await the Moshiach
And less-though-cognate sublunary aid
We line our wrongs into a cadenced march
As if each wrenching turn for the worse
Could not but appeal
To the theatrical sense
Of that-which-knows-we suffer
And create desire for resolution.

"Yes, but I will not let you go".
Until the poet at his pen,
The suicide, and Jews in Egypt
Project the insults they have borne
On their tormentors,
Rest from the hope of intercession,
And depart.

LOWELL

Gray as to walls, and gray as to the ceiling
Though it once was white
As snow in a painting of a milltown
When the river froze.
And gray as to the pressed-tin ceiling and
The runnelled Oak Floor.
Now: it would not burnish, so it could not shine
Along or resting on that still unnamed flow
Which drove the engines of the place.
We turned back, as who could then not,
To a snapped rotten snap which kept the skater on the bank
Til cries of men who rushed the ladder to the pond
When whose son disappeared.
With folly to shore up
The afternoon
If that well of self-pity announced itself deplete.
In something like respect.
Until the last day.
Until both sides
Of that silly fence
Were one. And until all of it was done.

In Memoriam Michael Merritt

Back in transition to a meadow
Nothing as literal as a deer on the pond
Nor empty as praise
Fought to support his claims.

Gnawed by the War, we reflect
in no hush of the posturing millennium
Nor bombing. Just the business of the world
Some beauty, and the coldest reason
Shaking the dross from itself.

BOULDER PUREY

Boulder Purey with the men and gods.
Cinched to the mast, though deaf,
we sift through memory like heathen Chinee
combing their excrement for rice.
Or Sixty-Ninth and Ellis — found
the kids on their knees, intent on the practice of ring taw.

To puff the spirits of that day,
and anomie by talisman.

The puissant Boulder Purey.
Boats in a green shed, that polio summer,
when they winched the behemoth submersible
athwart the Outer Drive,
boys lured in cars became dead
in the waste space a courtesy title had as
the Bird Sanctuary.
Youths stove in my head
while, kites and skates, two seasons on the Midway;
and neither the return of Houdini
nor the White Palace
but boys on the Wooded Island,
Jackson Park, the schoolyard,
Hot and Cold, Chicago, Illinois.

THE WATERWORLD

But did we not
Mint our excuse to sin,
And nurture it to our advantage?

Now here, now there,
Like drops on a pond
Shot by the needlegun
From the silt to the surface; now
The mechanism of our thought
Leaps in reverse
Like that hid engine of the waterworld.

Philosophers all, then we pray:

Goad us to acceptance,
Until our scoured resignation,
Bleached in loathing,
License our longing for revenge.

LABOR DAY

"Marah" from "bitter" In the prophet's tongue
Survived in the cartographer's cognomen and
The eponymous bitterness bequeathed us
Where the Cunard, Black Ball, White Star fortunes,
Swelled in the stench of steerage
In frenzy to strike the rock —
Once for luck, twice to insure exclusion
From the very Eden it proposed.

The white shirt pocket puked
Pencils and cigarettes.
The mailbox torso stuck on sausage legs,
He strode The Overpass,
Or took one during Little Steel,
In the perennial Red Scare that was the Industrial Age, until
Now not the Pinks, but the Tobacco,
Sent him to see Joe Hill.

Mountainous ashtrays on the
Cigarette-striped board
Across which my Bull glared at yours.
That brief rhodomontado
In the Labor Caanan.
Debs in the Joint. Bombmakers, Pamphleteers.
Big Bill, Haymarket Saints, axe-handles for the Goons
    at Pullman
In that hundred-years war
Til the scab from Orange County

Told the broken back of Labor.
That swine, punk of the FBI,
Informer, clown, and all his wranglers,
True to their code, the exudate upon the Crown
    of Thorns.

Sixteen-to-One, free Silver met the trickle-down
'Til never the brave homosexuality of our Nurse,
Nor the Brave Prairie Rose
Sang to the working class.

Where no tyke rushed the growler,
Where no evening-scrubbed paterfamilias
Donned his regalia for the Lodge.
No Darrow, no Debs, no,
"A man with a trade is a man, and he can tell
The rest of the world to go to Hell."

No sinner, no saint.
No Bryan, no Goons and Martyrs
Just the soft clicking of the keys
The Good Lord sent down to distract us
In the final moments of a life without work.

Labor Day 1992
(In memory of my father)

OLYMPIA

Surprised in the grace of the fat man's dance;
Or: though in honesty we allow each
Of the girl's individual features
Disappointed, the conglomerate pleased.

But it is not the girl, nor her companion,
Nor his inspirited step, nor her radiance.
Neither the thought, nor its amendation,
The diary, nor the pen,
Nor any apposite construction of the couple's burden.
Nor our ability to patronize the dance —
It is just the dance.

Song of the Sissies

No, I Am Sick Of The Whole Affair.
Meritless As A Tone-Poem,
That Interlude In The Barberchair,
That Fine Rhodomontade
Where Singly Worthless Images
Shine In Mechanical Eternity,
And We Denominate It God.
Meanwhile The Dutch And The Brody
For Who Rose From The Eames Chair
In Limitless Languorous Stages,
Noting The Dawn In The Park,
Sick Of The Whole Affair,
Went Screaming To And Happy From The Height,
Square With The World Which Bore Them,
Blessed By The One Remark:
No Doubt They Did As They Thought Right.

The Pond at Twilight

Vast black crows in the smoke yard
Mock the hand that sowed the field.
Dry summer or cold spring
Leached color from the Pond
The White Sign said at twilight:
"Do not pursue me, for I flee."
Incomprehensible, save we reflect
That it is not for Man.

Not in pursuit of food
But in idolatrous and awkward
Folly called understanding,
Now the faro box, or Politics
Lends that compulsion;
And the urge to husband energy,
Warped from the fight for food,
Impels our self predation
As the deer on the pond, barking alarm,
Torn down by dogs,
Dies screaming like a bad impulse;
Dry Summer or cold spring all one, incomprehensible
In the long overview of our attrition,
Save we reflect it is not for Man.

VA-ETZE

The bark which sheathed the wands
Was stripped, not as misunderstood,
To make a tunnel,
But to fashion Pipes of Pan.

Their music brought forth then a particolored face
Stained in the suppressed rage
Of the musician

Laban's sheep and Jacob's wage
And their contention
Lived in the mismade visage
Of an innocent race
Until the untold generation
Happy in ignorance,
Shone free of their quarrel.

R.

I loved the fact that you were sleeping.
On the couch lay with a book
Of their time
The while, waked in that atmosphere
When you go where
Then in your youth, to not retail
Exploits of our lost time,
Auditors equally deaf, in your age
to remember me.
Five hours on
We were parted
And stank in a two-day shirt
Always as you awoke
Perfect and pure,
Who appreciate, when I am in that sleep,
Then to those:
I loved you when you slept and
Those are five hours denied them.

BAD PENNY

Bad Penny
Coming Back
But Yet We Still Would View It With Affection

The Mysterious Healing Processes Of Grief
Like Punctuation In An Ancient Text,
Amharic Or The Thighs
Of The Nubian Goddess

Now But Our Bad Penny
On The Tongue Like Blood,
Derailed The Railroad Train

We Watched Like Frightened Gods
While The Vast Locomotive
Swelled To The Last Girth Of The World
Ravaged The Town

And Our Beloved Penny
On The Eyes Of Poets
Wasted From Egoism
By Administration Of That Coin

Whoever Controls Copper Rules The World

THE GRAPH

The vice voice of rectitude,
Like dinner with a drunk —
That deep mercantile truth:
Those we cured of the scurvy
Had not enjoyed it prior to our coming;
And the holy writ
An interesting mistranslation —
That one had done perfectly, so we should all do well.

Or whose son, in a savage satire on autism,
Opened his eyes, spoke
And rose to prominence bankrupting the middle class.
Who bequeathed eighty shades of mustardware
To a museum the halls of which stank of piss.

Abstracted and immortalized as reason
They rest on the porch cooled by their balance
Cursing inaction whilst the Jews heaved up the pyramids.

It drives the psychotic on
To further flights of self-aggrandizement
Until the cops beat the pimp,
Until the tower shivered on our heads
And good and bad alike
Retired, stunned, once more, to the wilderness
To contrive unity.

Two Colors

Blue herons on the pond,
So blue, Ashen-blue, almost white;
Not blue at all, really,
Not gray, not blue-gray —
Although you could say it —
But like ashes.
Blue by courtesy.

The American Kestrel.
Rufous on its back —
A bar of that orange
That passes for red in the wild.
Tenné, in the language of Chivalry —
Fox-red, *tenné*.

Eisenstein

Jose can you see
The death ray in the livingroom
Ration obscenity?
"The Rav!"
Out of the Far Turn
While the world
Voided its bladder on his back
And told him it was raining.
Removed from the Heron on the Pond
Are those two Instances of Jollity.
The broadcast seeds proclaimed
The meadow gone to red, to blue
In Indian Paintbrushes,
While the excise of the now-not-uttermost
Revealed they would habitate their aspect of the country,
And he —
Excising the soft toady, do you see?
Before exchange in Gossip,
Who had faced the Puritan in "fifties glee"
With that excess of character;

And, their lives lived,
Retired to die.
Jose. The question, as the Rav, as to the
Comfort of the Spectator,
From the French, To Assist,
At two essentially unique concours —
Who slapped my sister silly

In his gloss on the Korean War,
The two jokes, queried, who
Who are the Yellow Peril?
Who, for Trivia, was ruined by Cheap, Chinese Cheap
    Labor?
Who by the Molly MacGuires?
But the plague, when it comes,
However we've anticipated,
Is the stunning shock
Drove by the gap,
Of the electrical spark
To negate its bank, and
Jump to the New Assertion

In that orgasm — not thought —
Which, slack-jawed, and sick, then,
Exists as History.

POEM. DECEMBER. CABOT.

Japan tea in a metal cup
And thick moccasins froze
As the cherry smoke rose up
And then the Dese Dem Dose
Sought solace in it as it rose
The snow would not conceal the ground
Neither the sense wholly obscure the sound
Of the stick in the forest
Snapping the end-of-luck,
The cheap alarm, the end of rest,
The languid doe, the hidden buck,
Rock-hardened greasy shoes,
Chilled point of recollection; and
The jaundiced watermelon moon
Which shone
Upon the starving deer
The hungry town
And one
Noted it down
To close it down
And be shut of the year.

THE FRENCH AUTOMATON

The French Automaton — The Janissary
Of Sightless Fortune. Miracle Revealed.
Thespian Mamleuke, Constrained to Wield
Weapons of disingenuous display.

Spectators, likewise, from Component rest,
Jerked into life and marshaled toward the tomb
Enmotioned by we-know-not what behest,
Dance for the pleasure of we-know-not-whom.

(For Ricky Jay)

FELLOW

A chap
shepherded any number
of Jack Russell
terriers
Across the promenade.

Ô là, Monsieur le Prêtre
Que tu es drôle
'vec tes chaussures
de cuir d'Espagna et
tes pantalons si bruins.

They ruint the St. Cloud
as the twelfth
circle of hell was expanded
for architects.
Who would have thought juvenile
sex behind the Robie House
would license
this fine sensibility.

A judge of Israel
as Laban said
must delegate
his charge.

O fugitive
O full-completed
honeycomb.

The cap of the Chrysler Building
Mormon bees
make art for the dead queen
while in the Athens of the north
a chap shepherded
any number of
Jack Russell dogs
Athwart the Promenade.

THIS AND THAT

Some say this
And some say that
And some say an alleycat
And some say a fishing hat
And some say a hunting cap
And some say a coffeecup

Or wander in the store
Before
A serrated knife for grapefruit
Before typing paper
Or a juicer
or

An aeroplane
And the contents therein

An engine
Magazines
With pictures of
A watch, a dress, a building.
Men and women traveling and reading

One report read:
Increase the supply
of various supplies
Control the cost
And order all conditions
To our benefit.

One article showed how
To fix overly-salted soup
By the addition
Of potato.

In the store
A shopping cart
Stood by
To cradle this package or that
Against the ravages of gravity

The fishing hat
Bore on its crown
The proud medallion of a fly
A dog chased the alleycat.
The bold numeral SEVEN
Stamped in the brass tag
Hung on the collar on his neck

The plane
Flew over the man in the hunting hat.

Three generations sat
On mismatched windsor chairs
At breakfast.
Some said this and some said that

The dog's dish rested in the gloom
Beneath the table.
The cat's dish lay in a sunny corner of the room.

About the Author

David Mamet is the author of numerous award-winning plays, including *Glengary Glen Ross*, *Oleanna*, *Speed the Plow*, and *The Old Neighborhood*, as well as novels, essay collections, and books on the art and craft of writing and directing. His screenplay credits include *The Spanish Prisoner* and *House of Games* (both of which he also directed) as well as the Oscar-nominated *Wag the Dog*. He lives in Vermont.